Spiritual Awareness

Published by BooxAI

ISBN: 978-965-578-149-6

Spiritual Awareness

A Meaning of Life Guided by a Religion of Choice

Tina Suyas

CONTENTS

I. Life of the Author

I've come to believe that my life is a gift from God. I was blessed to be born, no matter the circumstances I faced. Though I've faced many trials and unfortunate situations, I've learned that how we grow up does not define who we are. Instead, it's the lessons we learn that move us forward and mold us into who we are meant to be. The future—those versions of us that have yet to be discovered, have already been designed and fashioned in the Spirit Realms, led by the faith and glory of God. Satan, the Great Deceiver, attempts to destroy your clarity and stain your belief in your Creator. He looks to sully the truth that God is the answer to all things. As you will see, I fully believe that there is only one certainty in life: death. So, until that day comes, I encourage all to accept the life you have and learn to live to the fullest. This way you can share the lessons you learn with others. Those lessons make up the design of your Creator. God aims to bring you closer to your purpose, not to mankind.

Throughout this book, I've collected the moments of my life that shaped me and the lessons I've learned through them all. My goal is to share my journey in this world and reveal the hope that exists for the hopeless. My experiences show how I've let go of the battle I've engaged in with Earth and embraced what so many have lost: the presence of God and his physical form. This is the awareness that God exists in the mind, brain, flesh, and soul of His creation. As you journey through these pages, connect with your soul deeper than before, and open yourself to the exploration of life. Seek God's meaning for you. I pray these stories will help you reach enlightenment. God bless.

II. Epiphany 35

I was 35 years old when I had a dream. Like an old film projector, my life up to that point was flashing in chronological scenes, moving through each decade of my past in a rapid fashion. Throughout this experience, my past self was in conversation with my future self—the version of me I hadn't met yet. This was a surreal experience.

With every moment I witnessed, I began to teach myself the challenges and struggles I overcame. I witnessed my power in a real way. Slowly, I felt myself becoming enlightened to the strength and sheer endurance I had possessed, and yet, never quite realized. It was as if I was shaking hands with tomorrow. The conversation with my future self turned from awareness to instruction. Suddenly, this time traveler was telling me how to continue healing and fully overcome the pain that I had carried for so long.

Suddenly, my attention turned to my surroundings. I found myself floating in a red pool of liquid. It wasn't thin like water, but rather it was a sea of blood. Frightened by where I was, I yelled to my future self, asking if this was real.

Suddenly, my strength began to wane, and I found myself drowning in this strange ocean. My future self suspended above me, told me that what was, in fact, drowning me was the emotions of sorrow and confusion that had held me captive from my past. I was gasping for air. She continued speaking, unfazed by my struggles. She told me that God had brought me this far and He would continue to carry me through the rest. It was my obedience that kept me connected to His protection. I chose a life of faith, and that was the raft by which I had survived this pain for so long. She then reminded me to believe in the version of life I had wanted to live. To chase my passion and be the woman of courage and faith that God had built me to become, driven by His wisdom, and the wisdom of His Earth.

This all sounded great, but still, I was drowning, struggling to breathe. The struggles had me bound and were dragging me beneath this Red Ocean. She then reminded me that it was the influences I had allowed to fill my mind and soul that were beginning to control and change my destiny.

The scenes were still dancing in front of me. I watched how in every decade, every scene, there were moments where I was alone, with no one to talk to in my life but myself. The irony was thick. Here I was, gasping for air, dying in shame and worry, and yet still, carrying a conversation with myself. Finally, I captured a stride. I began to swim forward. Where to—I wasn't sure. But it kept me afloat, so I swam. She was there, watching me flail as I continued the struggle. Suddenly, like a wind in my ear, I heard the voice of God whisper:

"Tina, you have always had me. I'm with you, in your soul. Trust me, and let me carry you. You've allowed your freedom to be stripped from you. You're struggling."

I kept swimming, listening to the voice of my Creator.

"I've come to bring you back to where you belong. You've been too busy, too distracted. It's while you're sleeping that I have your full attention."

It was nice to know I was dreaming, but the struggle and fight were all too real. So, I kept swimming.

God continued, "I saw you cry your last tears when your father died. I watched as your soul flooded out, and you were left empty, hollow. I brought you peace through the battle."

Suddenly, the first decade of my life was shown. I watched as a much younger version of myself was shown.

"You chose me at a young age, Tina," God whispered. "You found me and held on to me. You became a lesson to your mother and embodied the Love of your father. He chose me to have me, and He showed you to me."

Like a fast-forwarded movie, I watched as God showed me the influence of my father. As a young child, my dad gave me confidence. He instilled wisdom and faith in me, molded me, and protected me. Next, I was shown my second decade. Center screen, my father was there, leading me to God, where I made my commitment. Though troubled and with many setbacks, I grew and learned through the influence of my father. Then, like clockwork, the scene changed again.

"It's here, in your third decade, Tina, where you finally gave in to me," God explained. "I've watched you so closely. You've been taken for granted by those you loved. The purity of your heart has dreadfully misguided you, taking you down paths you were never meant to follow. But yet you still have the courage to believe in me, despite it all. I'm proud of you, Tina."

I found myself crying, still treading water. The words stung deeply. My life, scrolling by before my eyes, and the realization of my destiny became overwhelming. But through the struggle of it all, clarity was forming. Like puzzle pieces, the dream began to make sense. This was a wake-up call. A re-direction. A Repositioning.

"I forgive you for blaming me, Tina, for taking your father away from you. But know He stands guard from above. He protects you, even now. He wants you to know he's proud of you. He loves you, and he's honored to have been a part of this story. Your Father showed you how to be fierce, but now he asked you to find your peace. He's with me, preparing a place for you."

I began to feel healing in my soul. Strength was pouring into my blood connections, and I felt the relationships I chose with others along this journey of life began to mend.

I cried out to God, "I've stayed true to you, God! I've given you my heart! I've had to forgive myself for those three decades of my life. The last seven years of this life have been too brutal. I need your healing! I'm broken, God, inside and out. I'm watching these scenes, witnessing my old self torn to shreds. My flesh is aching, and my heart is dying. I'm hollow, God. Please, help me! I can't bear this alone! I've been betrayed, deceived, and overlooked by those I love. My world is, in reverse, chaotic. I've tried to heal so many, and I've forgotten to heal myself! I've come back to you, to improve my life. To learn from the lessons you've given me. You promised to guide me, my daughter, and my descendants. I want my legacy to be known through my experiences, not my words. I want people to remember my actions and be encouraged to believe in You. To believe in themselves!

I turned and faced my future self. She was still suspended, watching as I struggled in the sea.

I pleaded, "Tell me, how can I move forward? Why are you only showing me this beautiful child I was and this current state of my third decade? What is next?"

And then it dawned on me. I realized that I needed to go back to my true belief. This child I saw before was a blessing, a miracle in the midst of madness. I saw how I learned through it all and was molded through it all. But I lost her along the way. I couldn't deal with the pressures and sorrow. I kept her clothes and went to her church, but in reality, I lost my ability to love.

"Tell me, future self. Why am I unable to believe in Love anymore?"

She came forward and leaned in. With a graceful voice, she began to teach.

"I'm here to tell you the lesson of it all, Tina. Move forward, and never stop swimming. It's the steady movement that will keep you from drowning in all of this. Aim for the shore ahead of you. You'll awaken soon."

So, I did just that. I swam. Moving through the sorrow and the shame. I found strength within that I thought I had lost. I made it through and reached the sand. As I slowly drifted from dreamscape to reality, I heard the voice of God one last time:

"Let go of it all. The test is over."

III. Conformity

As I have evolved, I've learned to choose individuality. Raised amongst a fractured representation of faith: a father who believed in God and a mother who practiced voodoo, concepts like identity and personal faith were unclear. What was clear, however, was the environment that seemed to press in on me as I grew. Until the age of 16, I spent my most vulnerable years in the company of my mother. In her community, there were two options for life: sell drugs or be on drugs. She sold them. In many ways, she served as an agent of chaos.

At eight years old, I experienced sexual and physical assault at the hands of a drug dealer who had business with my mother. This was a time of confusion. Being so young and innocent to the ways of evil, I couldn't separate the difference between support and abandonment. Yet even then, I was left to work through the pain myself. I learned, early on, the value of resilience, of holding tight to your own identity in the face of overwhelming circumstances. My mother, a product of her own choices and environment, resented me for this. Time and time again, I chose to survive. I chose to not cave into the pressure of the evil that surrounded me. This not only secured my soul, but it built a deep chasm between my mother and me.

It was shortly after I turned 16 that my mother forcibly emancipated me. I chose not to yield to her ways, and because of this, her last resort was to remove me entirely. A high schooler nearing adulthood, I was left alone–once again abandoned because of my resilience. You see, despite my upbringing, I gravitated toward my rhythm. This divinely appointed trait has led me to become the person I am today. I don't lean towards a certain "law" or hinge upon a set belief. I lean on truth, the word of God–the true power of the divine. I listen to the Universe–hear it speak.

But still, the only thing that remains attached is my understanding of the Dark Side of Reality. Because of my childhood, and the many trials I've faced since, I've adapted and developed the ability to master the Darkside–overcome the evil within that lurks in the shadows–and live radiantly in the light of God.

I've come to obtain, through my relationship with the Almighty, a very profound understanding of what is required, what is obedience, and what is self-respect. There are three distinct areas of life: the things we must do, the actions we choose to do, and the areas of our life that we respond to out of protection and respect for ourselves. As a child, we must absorb the wisdom that is projected from our roots. As we reach our pre-teen stage in life, we unconsciously choose to follow family traditions with respect to our elders. This is the moment in which habits are formed. This is due to the mental afflictions caused by a lack of ability at this age range to understand life for ourselves. Then, as teenagers, we strive to live free from rules to pursue a lifestyle of choice. In this stage, the teenager lacks the knowledge of accountability based on the choices made in their life.

Often absent from parenthood is remaining accountable to the hindsight we have of when God gave us nudges. Parents are often trapped in the specific area of childhood where the lessons God meant to give us were blocked. Often when an adult is in a child-like mentality, it's a result of broken emotional voids that hinder adult decisions, bringing consequences. A consequence is not always receiving bad things that happen to you. Karma is far more of a well-rounded term than that. It's used to distinguish the effect of the consequence you face.

Regarding bad karma, it's the cycle of the world lesson you did not heed. The phase of Mercury Retrograde, it's a period where we learn to govern our emotions and remain steadfast in our decision, not returning to the past.

When you receive good karma, your life is rewarded abundantly. For religions, it's a choice dictated by traditions. There aren't any U.S. churches that raise awareness of this, especially in a diversely accepted understanding. We read in the Bible,

"Appeal to you, therefore, brothers, by the mercies of God, to present your bodies as a living sacrifice, holy and acceptable to God, which is your spiritual worship. Do not be conformed to this world, but be transformed by the renewal of your mind, that by testing you may discern what the will of God is, what is good and acceptable and perfect." *Romans 12: 1-2*

"For I long to see you, that I may impart unto you some spiritual gift, to the end ye may be established." No matter what the situation, trust in God to follow his earth angels to guide you." *Romans 1:11*

In my adult life, it's become clear that my greatest strength is to not conform to anything that will push me out of the light of the Lord and away from what is required, obeyed, and respectful of myself. If my soul doesn't agree–even yearn– then I can't move. The world around us–and within us–is constantly absorbed by the darkness that surrounds us–yet choosing to believe and follow your purpose in this life over all other paths is how you conquer the battle with conformity.

IV. The Mustard Seed

I have, firsthand, learned the difference between having faith and losing it. Growing up in a home that did away with its true form and replaced it with self-serving, evil replacements, I had to choose the way of the Creator. Learning from His word and the actions recorded in the history of His people, I chose forgiveness. This is the small, mustard seed-sized faith spoken of in the New Testament. A choice to lean on the small piece of faith we all have, hidden deep within, that bids us to choose wholesome and righteous acts over worldly influence.

This journey is not fleeting–or a passive "flavor of the day" exercise, but rather a rite of passage. It's, at times, treacherous to find others who pursue truth over lies. Yet, if you are willing to be truthful with yourself and exercise that small bit of inherited faith within, you can find the meaning of life–and all its grandeur.

We must remember that God is the Creator of all things. And our line of communication is the prayer we pray to Him. Even in the unknown or unspoken words we pray, He listens. He takes them into consideration and offers forgiveness. We must always exercise this small, deeply hidden faith in order to allow His will to push us forward. If we give Him the opportunity, He will use us to perform His word on Earth and guide others through the understanding we will obtain. I have yielded to my ultimate design: a vessel of God on this Earth. And through His power, I'll rise above the dimension I have come from and enter the dimension in which He resides. The scripture tells us,

"And He *said to them, "Because of the littleness of your faith; for truly I say to you, if you have faith the size of a mustard seed, you will say to this mountain, 'Move from here to there,' and it will move; and nothing will be impossible to you." *Matthew 12:20*

"The apostles said to the Lord, "Increase our faith!" And the Lord said, "If you had faith like a mustard seed, you would say to this mulberry tree, 'Be uprooted and be planted in the sea,'; and it would obey you." *Luke 17: 5-6*

V. Eye of the Soul

My home and my foundation rest within my soul. My life is driven by the guidance that comes from my pineal gland, also known as my third eye. It's from here that I derive the strength needed, like the faith protruding from a mustard seed, to find joy on the rainy days and relief from wounds and aches left from the beatings of life. My accomplishments have been crafted, and my prayers have been answered through conversation with God. Now, I live my life as a shining example of just how wonderful it can be to believe in God and yourself. The rest of life is just a lesson. Something that must be taught before you are able to enjoy a fruitful lifestyle. You must look at *who* you are first so that you can accept yourself fully. You must learn who you were created to be so that you can judge yourself appropriately. It's not through the control of others that we operate. Only by God's design. We find each other and view each other as different wavelengths. Some vibrations go together, and others do not. Accompany yourself with like-minded people. My tribe is full of like-minded people that clearly see we are gifted to teach others.

The rest of life is just a lesson to be learned before you can enjoy a fruitful and exhaling lifestyle. Look at what you are accepting for yourself prior to judging anyone. No one is in control of anyone else's decisions. It's about taking account of oneself. When a person becomes spiritually aware of the gifts bestowed by God unto them, it changes how they view life and interpret its essential meaning. I was given a great deal of insight into life at the early age of 10. As a child, I was fascinated with humanity in its entirety. I believe the Earth is like your mind. When your environment is cloudy, conflicted, and dark, you are not on your journey. I learned to read auras, numbers, moons, and energy vibrations.

These practices became the core of my apple tree. I am now rebuilding myself with Oreo cookies, wine, and coffee. I'm guarding the tenderness of my heart. I can be adaptable, and cordial. But I won't sugarcoat anything that I learn while healing.

As I discover the meaning of life, I strive to speak only what is necessary. When I began to read about the anthology, poets, numerology, mysticism, and child psychology, these studies helped me to understand how to adapt to a world full of the unaware.

When you accompany yourself with like-minded people, the lessons learned could be beneficial for growth and heighten your understanding. For the members of my soul tribe, I am honored to be amongst the elite people of humanity. The world is in desperate need of our gifts. We are called to heal our nation from self-destruction.

VI. C.O.M.A.: Cognizance, Observation, Mindfulness, Attentive

It's frightening at first to be aware of your status, amongst others. During the time spent induced in my coma, I was given true cognizance of my past life moments. This cognizance, or awareness, was necessary for me to heal from the burden often caused by the emotional, psychic gifts that have been bestowed upon me. Over time I have developed the innate ability to communicate telepathically with my ancestors. They've spoken to me both verbally and through colors and continue to show me things. In my moment of cognizance, they made me aware of times so powerful from my past that it brought me to tears. During that observation, I was placed in a physical form of complete stillness–unlike anything I had felt before. My flesh was cold, and my body was as solid as an oak tree. I could go nowhere but remain in my position. It was here I was introduced to mindfulness beyond any comparison. An opening of my mind to truths beyond my finite ability to fully comprehend. At the end of my mindfulness, I then transitioned to an awakening. I began to shed tears, realizing just how much God was battling me. I felt like Jacob in the Book of Genesis 32:22-32. The past I had walked through, lived through, and experienced, I realized then, was so like Jacob's. Struggle, despair, and overcoming.

In my family, I was the last edition of struggle and pain. The Love I yearned for so much was absent from them. My anger manifested and grew, eventually leading me miles away from my family. I witnessed a level of matriarchal power and control that gave way to oppression. Running far from the pain, I had to arrive at a place where I was attentive to Him and not to man. God removed me from destruction. As I journeyed, he held fast to me. When I lost my focus, he would carry me. My hip was broken at the socket, and I was placed in a weakened form. This gave way for God to show mercy for the life I asked to live. I thanked God and asked for His forgiveness. God answered my prayer and said to go towards the blessing He had bestowed upon me.

The swirling visions of past moments and physical pain, God's guidance, and ancestral telepathy came to an end when I was awakened by the voice of a woman named Lillian. She was the doctor who took me off life-support. A blue tube *was* pulled out of my mouth, and I was given a chance to live a long life with my beautiful child. I have been awake for eight years and nine months strong, living daily to raise awareness in the world. To God be the glory! I shall continue to be patient and know, through God, all blessings shall reign upon me. I know that part of my existence is to deliver a message of healing to anyone who has suffered loss or dealt with a coma.

VII. Awakening

"Grand rising," not *"good morning."* Every day, while you're above the ground, you are blessed by planting your feet atop the grass or within the sand. Allow yourself time and space to enjoy nature. Revel in it every time the sun rises. Think of those you know who can no longer witness its grand design. Embrace it. When the night falls, before ending your day, pray and give thanks for all you have experienced, and pray for a chance to see another day. Look forward to another chance to conquer what you are here to conquer. Pray for the wisdom and courage to fulfill the purpose you have while living above the ground.

Always take the time to enjoy nature, for it has, for so long, been misinterpreted. Nature is not a closure or ending to life. Instead, everything in it has room to feel its purpose, and it's that feeling that giveaway to the sound of nature we enjoy. Become one with your surroundings. Think: *why does the human body consist of 70% water?* Questions like this take some longer than others to answer. But it's not hard. We just need to know how to bend the air and enjoy each breeze. Outside of your body, what is life *beyond* the normal temperature? If death is permanent, why is life permitted? You are allowed to learn these answers. But the only way to receive them is to strengthen your relationship with the Creator. It's through him that you will be connected to your ancestors. And it's through your ancestors that you will be guided to the answers that you seek.

VII. Light of Dawns Darkness

(a poem)

From birth, it's been darkness. There is no light to see nor a tunnel to follow. It was God giving me a chance to grow incubated.

Throughout my life, I always wonder what life is. How are our minds programmed to function? This curiosity brought me into developing the place from childhood, youth, teenager, and adulthood.

I wasn't supposed to make it past my 1st year of life. I was told I would never be able to bear a child.

In the absence of directions, I maternally believed in the world wholeheartedly as a child. My paternal guidance did its best by giving me hope in myself through understanding, spiritually, I am destined to be here for the example of God's miracle.

As a youth, I knew the art of survival was about adoption and conformity. As a teenager, I was ready to align my self-discovery of what I saw with my human eyes. I began to enter adulthood during my pre-teen years. Due to my choices, I was abandoned by all maternal directions.

IX. New World Order

What causes a child to ask the question, "why?" It's the curiosity that forms by what they see and the directions they are given to follow. Our children are our examples. What becomes of their life is often dictated by what we have not healed from in our own past lives. Healing isn't only needed from a physical bruise. A damaged mind remains often damaged until the question of "why" is answered. Whenever we hear the question "why" from our children, it's simply the direction of God reminding His people and empowering His creation, to question the world and follow Him. The mind will rest once His direction is followed. It's in His written words that you will find your compass to live. In 2022, there is no human on this Earth who can deny God is real. As humans, we have seen His power. It's time to live now and embody the power granted to you. You can build a better world around you.

My courage in Spirit is the essence of God. I will enjoy my design by conforming to His direction and encouraging others to believe. Tomorrow, I will live within God by standing against segregation. We must write about the segregation that threatens us from living within our power. We must reach others with this wisdom. The New World Order is becoming aware that He lives within the Spirit of man.

X. Guidance for Children

What is a child's place, exactly? I have heard this question throughout my life. I've always wanted to show children where they fit in with life. I never remained silent when I knew the truth of something. No matter what brought on my curiosity, I chose to seek out the facts. Once I knew the facts, I felt safe knowing I had a place of comfort. I was able to construct my own life through the knowledge gained and the truths I connected to. I often spoke with elders, in which I found great joy. I then shared my knowledge by teaching other children. Though it is important to learn proper life skills, it is an even greater blessing to show others.

By age 13, I began applying the skills I learned. The fundamental lessons of cooking and cleaning were among the most key skills I utilized. I landed a job at 16, realizing the importance of using my skills to build the life I wanted to live. I never knew how much I had missed while being a kid until I worked 8 hours a day on the job. All the tasks I had to do were the same as a child, yet this time I was getting paid for them. It was fun to have freedom, but I didn't understand the full power of work until I was placed in the world.

My elders spoke of the freedom that came for them through hard work. I learned to apply this to every part of my life. Through my habits and treating hard work as stepping stones, my freedom in finances moved from home to a larger reality. The world is full of many capabilities. Following my dreams, I stayed focused as

I grew up. I never forgot what was said to me or shown to me. I looked at my life through a child's eyes.

My advice for children is to follow their dreams. Stay humble through all stages of life. It is through wisdom that you can take your next step forward. Your history is there to teach you and remind you of the lessons you received from others.

The cognitive ability under the age bracket of 18 is a presentation for adult immaturity. Children need the ability to think and speak their minds with tact and clarity to understand. When a child is sheltered from their voice, they are blocked from comprehension and suffer abuse both physically and mentally.

Pray for patience and guidance through the stages of development. It's imperative to prevent adults from having immature behavior and refusing to mentally accept their actions. It's about growth in cognitive accountability. They should be able to handle responsibility in their life. Children need emotional maturity in their life to be effective in communicating their emotions. When they don't have this in their life, they suffer from psychological deficits. Because childhood is the shortest span of life, it is the most effective focal point to nurture and guide them through the rest of their life in this world.

XI. Literature Inspired Me
(Tribute to Prof. Bernabe)

Professor's passion for teaching

My answers come from my experiences. In my life, I learned to enhance educational fundamentals in order to teach and, ultimately, reach my students. I aimed to show them ways to discover the truth in their own lives. My background in teaching the basics stems from teaching middle school, high school, and now college-bound students. In the past, I saw that the most extraordinary self-discovery I made was hell. What was so often lost was a person's mind in realizing their direction. Teaching youth encourages me to fine-tune the basics of literature: what is proper and what is structure. Some of the most significant contributions were teaching them about perspective and point of view.

When I began my career in high school, my focus shifted to comprehension. When I moved my career into college instruction, it came to my attention that students lost their past knowledge of literature by no longer reading. It's a unique experience to teach students the value of a book. By high school, this understanding can be lost in the drive to find themselves in this world. Yet once life happens, a student may discover themselves back in college. They may look to learn a trade, but no matter the trade, the key to anything rests on the value of reading.

Reading provides clarity; answers for what they need the most in life. It was always in a book for me. And my first book was the Bible.

XII. Forgiveness

When we learn to accept our actions, we must learn to forgive the actions of others. To forgive someone, we must first see the reflection in the mirror. We must understand who we are. Only then can we identify the wrong in others. Here is where we find out how to respond. Should we repent or bring death to the situation?

I spent a lot of time in unforgiveness before I realized it was all an illusion. It's a false truth to discover that a moment was not real. I wasn't real to myself. Love heals over time, but it's not real until you love yourself just as much as you have loved others. With dedication and endless sacrifice, a moment of forgiveness to yourself allows Love to enter, which then turns into everlasting life. You are your own best soulmate in life. When two souls can first forgive and love themselves, they can then heal together and build a long-lasting life. It is then that their life is strengthened through the admiration that they see in each other, as individuals of this shared feeling called Love.

I'm blessed with a spiritual sense that heightens my five common senses. Through spirituality, I can see my past, present, and future images of me in this world. In the past, I didn't forgive those who hindered my mental clarity and kept me from how I truly felt at that time. This was consuming me in the present. So, I went out on a journey of solitude to bring peace to myself. I first forgave myself for the things I was unable to see. As the blinds have been lifted, I have released it all and put some respect on my name.

XIII. Mental Therapy Objection

When it comes to clarity, is it not from a sound mind to decide? The mind is a vessel in which all the absorption someone perceives is trapped. When the mind is blurred, the action someone takes is based on the thought they had.

It's because of this that I believe the importance of mental therapy is monumentally scarce worldwide. It's embedded that in order to receive therapy, you must first be insane. I beg that officials and leaders see this issue as is. There is no doubt the suffocation of humanity continues to increase because the world lacks support for those who are in need.

For one to not become a product of their environment, the mind needs therapy to transform. In therapy, a person learns to rediscover themselves through acceptance and understanding. It's with a lack of knowledge that they made wrong choices instead of the right choice for their life. I find it very therapeutic to realize that the basics of life begin with the power of reading. When someone begins to seek therapy for anything, the mind may experience friction. A therapist may then suggest journaling your emotions. This is an exercise that allows someone to contend with mental anguish. Through this tactic, a person can reveal what makes sense and what doesn't, and, ultimately, what their next course of action should be. If it's not on my mental level, it must go. I'm only accepting what is serving me through divine guidance. I'm proud of my accomplishments and have achieved so much through the choice of choosing myself. I never had a saga in my life. I'm going after the fulfillment brought by realizing who Tina is.

Truly for self-growth, I speak from experiences that can be a conflict in times when my weakness would present an illusion that would take up my time. I don't want the past, as I affirm. I am who I am. I am over the abuse and lack of intellectual stimulation, not just the flesh.

XIV. PEACE

The true definition of the word "peace" is *the ability to trust that the Creator himself is always with you by your side through everything.* No one should fear their circumstances. The Creator has a message behind any situation, even if it saddens the person who faces it. When a person gets to a point in life where there is no peace, or there is no movement from the Creator, this is a lesson you are learning. We call this a tribulation. It's here that a person can arrive at a breakdown of life due to the absence of the Creator. But the Creator doesn't live within that person. Instead, the Creator finds a way to reach that person and provide peace through experiencing nature.

<u>Earth's communication channels:</u>

- Trees are the roots of your spinal connection to the Earth.
- Branches carry burdens.
- Leaves fall once a year. This is the season to harvest.
- Snow is a moment in time to be alive and frozen. To fear to bear the storm.
- Rain cleanses your Aura.
- Thunder awakens enlightenment from the shadow of the moon.

- Hurricanes are our emotions that are at war. Cast them into the seas.
- Grass absorbs your aches like a bandage to a wound.
- Sun blessings come every sunrise to continue your walk in the journey of life.
- The moon is within the epicardium.
- Stars are hope floating on aspiration.
- The ocean is the constant flow of emotions.
- Dirt is the natural fertility to replenish.

XV. The Journey Begins

From the beginning of my life, I was curious to discover what else life was all about. As a child, I observed parts of my life as lessons. With my first experience, I quickly chose not to be a product of my environment. I refused to allow false truth to control my life throughout my adolescence. I saw that the way out of my troubled childhood was to join the military after high school. It was here that I was able to fully understand my abilities and grow in independence. A hunger for self-accomplishments manifested in me, and I pursued success in life. While in service, I gained the cognitive enhancement needed to progress forward with confidence in myself.

<u>Affirmation of self to say daily:</u>

- I am attracting everything I need.
- My concepts are profitable thoughts.
- I am aware of my higher self.
- I push toward my own definition of life.
- I love you, Tina. Go for it.
- Smile and exhale. Every breath is a chance to conquer your quest to explore life.

- Don't let the clock beat you. Move forward in your cycle of life.

- Don't let the clock beat you. Move forward in your cycle of life.

XVI. Self-Reflection

I choose to be present at the moment. I am what I have conquered through healing. I have become who I am by overcoming the unknown and climbing the unbearable mountains and treading the treacherous rivers and oceans in my life. I am replenished with self-awareness of the tribulations that I overcame. I am stronger because of the many lessons that are repeated within myself.

Until you master who you are from the inside out, what is felt in the core sheds light on the outer appearance. It's a radiant light that God places over you to see a higher self looking back at you, opposite of the shadow from your past where darkness is trapped. This is why the past tense is not present. Instead, it's history to learn from. I have witnessed the damage my mind has endured. For what is constantly cloudy is seeking a way out into the open. My past struggles are trying to silence my mind. But I spark the flame and let the herbs feed my mind. My soul is floating within me, and I am absent from the flesh. In my soul, I transport to other dimensions just to escape. My flesh is numb due to the pain. The higher I drift, the more I must isolate myself from the surroundings that try to hurt me.

I'm greeted by my ancestors, who remind me to allow God's light to expel me. I need to speak to the unspoken. I need to hear the world yearn for mental equality. I need to support others as I learn from my experiences. I need to use my life as a compass for others. In every direction, there is a life lesson, and through the lesson, you find out the end result. Do you choose yourself, or do you choose God?

As I came to terms with this question in my mind, I began to seek answers biblically. If I only pray at my altar and express to God all my truths; if I ask for forgiveness as I seek out to follow His guidance by aligning myself through the books I read; if I recite and remind myself that through God, all can be healed, then it's only a matter of time my tears will dry, and my frown is turned into a smile. Then my shout will rise after the thunderstorm. Looking forward to the vision of making my present, I will realize that my future self has awakened from the womb. I'm detaching from the past and creating a better version of myself. What you see humanly is not who I am. I am the color purple. I am number 11. I am the first goat of my generational heritage. My stripes are black and white, and the power that lives within me makes the most out of life. I seek peace for the world. Once you follow your purpose, you then become enlightened.

Is it not true to mind your own business? Your purpose is derivative from God to you. It's a program inside a person's mind. The personal relationship with God is your guidance alone. The vessels of angels on Earth are in your life by God's directions to help you align with them. It is helpful here if you take the initiative to seek out and know it's ok to ask for mental help. There is no such thing as anyone's life not mattering to someone. Everyone has a purpose and a call to fulfillment to God.

In some form fashion, it's best to communicate blockages that are hindering your ability to live a life ordained for you. Seek the wisdom and courage to live life. With every sunlight, you are blessed to live another day, and at night you should pray that morning shall once again reign upon you to try again. The chances to live life are endless through the breath of God that He blows inside of you. Cherish the seconds that you are able to feel your heartbeat. Never lose touch with God, for He is the hope and the power to make anything that hinders you be removed for your betterment.

XVII. Service to Others

I understood that teaching one another is liberating. The reward of teaching and paying it forward is to assist the Creator of the world Himself. We share amongst others, and in doing so, we gain relief from the congestion and suffocation of the world we as humans share. Until we come in contact fully, the mission of God is that we are placed here to rejoice in life with people that have the same goals. Purpose and direction come when one forms a personal relationship with God. Only then will their responses come in the whispers of the wind. The sudden hesitation that one feels before one embarks on this journey could be counted against one if they don't move forward. The time is now to put forth the awareness of spirituality and religion. To provide the guidance that drives discovery in life.

I'm speaking from my own firsthand experiences. It's not enough to wait until destruction comes. Life is certain to end, but it's what we do with every second we have that matters the most.

XVIII. Embracing God's Gift

The gift from God to humanity comes as you wish. What drives a person is a result of what that person follows. This could be any form of tradition. Though it may be confirmed, it isn't the will of God. It's best to do better as you learn better. Seek the wisdom He places in the death of your soul. A person must seek Him to find the purpose of their life. We are here on this Earth to complete God's creation. The guidance is written in 66 books combined and the man it speaks of. The number 66 means guidance from angels. This guidance provides humanity with insight into our lives. When you see the number 66, it holds a double meaning—double the guidance that the angels are sending.

The 6th signifies balance and stability. Together, 66 speaks of compassion, generosity, and determination. Sixty-six is overall a healing sign that teaches us to understand the essence of unconditional Love. The greatest provision given to the heart will be delivered by the Holy Spirit.

In the absence of Love, one can be consumed with hatred. But, when you embrace the gift of God, you're overcoming the error of every challenge that's present in your life. Self-love and obedience give way to His will, and that'll deliver you with an abundance of blessings.

XIX. Congratulations

Rejoice, for my name is God. I am the Creator. Your wish is cast upon my command, as you have survived and stood up to every test of time unphased. With the Love of God in your heart, you spent your life believing and growing through me. I shall show you just how special you are and why you are a child of mine. In the past, you admitted you needed me. And now, you gave in to me and my way by abiding by the directions written in the Bible. The knowledge of how life was created that I shared with you. And today, you live in your future by having no worries. Your wealth is rewarded by divine timing.

My soul is at peace now. To you, I shall give all the glory. I overcame to fully commit to you. And now, with self-awareness, I will finish what I started. At every step, you took me and held my hand. I smile with a pride that is shielded by my confidence in knowing you are there. Throughout my childhood, I made it through. I survived the Army. I survived battles back home, even after the wars I fought in. In the blink of an eye, I am passing through my 30s, unbothered and untroubled. At 38, I am chasing after every moment I'm blessed to have grown from. To God, I thank you for the destruction of my past that gave way to rebuilding me in your armor. I carry a torch of faith. I'm walking out early and into the light called Heaven on Earth. Salute to self-discovery. Congratulations, you made it!

XX. She is my F.I.R.E.

The sound of her voice fills me up. Her voice is my flame. I move accordingly as God directs the last beat and breath of my being. Raising you are the best moments in this life I have lived. I'm announcing my throne to you. You are the precious value to my legacy. I give you the wisdom of my memories of the life I have learned. I leave you with Love beyond the infinite nature of time. Your life means that only God can give you the answers that you seek out of curiosity. The questions you have for your interests in life as you grow older. Thank you for being a part of the focal point in my life. I am truly honored to be blessed with the best part of me. Continue to pray for anything that you wish to know or need to have a better understanding from God to guide you in your actions. Always remember I love you the most. My strength has been your courage.

XI. Love Cycle

After you reach Love for self, understand how to love yourself, and know what's best for you, the lesson learned manifests in when you choose to love another. A narcissistic person is someone who has broken into you to manipulate you into being a person who is a giver to them, handing over all that you dream and desire for yourself.

My Love is a reflection of self-growth and empowerment. I'm more than sex. I always tell the truth about my own actions and accept me. The tower moments that redirected me to loving myself have developed my life into becoming the wise one to build with. I'm not built to be any human stepping stone or security while they lack stability. What is the point of attraction when it's misinterpreted in relationships? A lover's process with envy leads to obsession and addictions that must be tarnished. For every single person who tried to take advantage of me, I ask you to shine the sunlight on those individuals. I have learned of my Love as I began to cut off those in that season. I choose not to have anyone in my life that uses me to kill your voice in me, God.

It's the people who are here that are absent and just know who they are. I want new Love and the innocence of someone I could spend life exploring together. My vision of true Love is going to be illuminated. Bland foods are off. I am living in my truest form with self-identity. God reveals reasons why people are in my life. According to the guidance I am given, I move. It's draining to know how much I wanted your energy. I don't connect with your emotional immaturity and manipulation you have had for more than 20 years of my life. I am accepting my part and my mistakes.

XXII. Sage & Jane

A Capricorn's ego. We are fighters who are determined to challenge ourselves. To achieve the highest of life and to gain a relationship with God until we learn our life purpose. We have the devil in bed with our emotions that are governed by the moon. Our power is analyzed through past relationships in all aspects of life sustainability. Remove yourself from people who stay on the path that is their own.

I am my own authentic self. I am disciplined. I am in charge of my nine cups. He gives us life. We praise through all our battles. I have learned this from my personal experiences in the United States Army as a part of Operation Iraqi Freedom from 2006 to 2007. This was my first battle. I was injured and stayed in until October 2009. My second battle was becoming a federal contractor in December 2009. My career ended with a traumatic accident. This was my third battle. I was reconstructed with an armor of God's implants of metal. I am walking on a purpose to seek out what is my true definition.

My phone was broken. Our lease is where we focus, and I replenish. I'm humble through all my blessings. You don't need to go through everything in the Bible to understand what is meant for you. To know God is real, you relate your life through your curiosity and search understanding of what life means to you. Go seek out prescriptions for the guidance that is written for you to follow. It takes time, perseverance, and faithfulness.

XXIII. Moment 4 Life

I stand on this island, awaiting your arrival. I plan to go off the current study, but the waves are too hot for me to see you. I'm jumping in the air to allow my daughter to show you the light of the way to me. To see the foundation that builds from what is bonded by the D.N.A. we made from poverty. Basse in the Aura of peace. See that this is the beginning of your 4 Life moments. Welcome home, Carmen.

XXIV. Pulse

My self-awareness is the beat to my rhythm. I hear the pulse pounding. It's like my feet see the mountain rock beneath me as I am chipping away at the boulder. I push with perseverance my way up to the top of the world called Heaven on Earth. Thunder is like a heartbeat. Every tick of every thump is a blink of an eye. Exhale his freedom. Darkness is self-slavery imprisonment.

A virtuous icon. The row model of self-sufficiency. I love myself with green abundance through your answers. As a wise woman, I cherish Bible lessons. The pep talks.

And best of all is my spiritual teacher. It's been eleven years of consistent Love and admiration. You are truly a gift from God in my life. By Steve and Solomon, the son of David, the greatest lesson of life you taught me was in reading to understand what it means to fear the Lord. Proverbs 31, I study and apply to my life daily and strive to live in my own truth, confidence, and faith. What is pleasant and protected by the Almighty. I have upgraded, even more, fasted through forgiveness, and I have finally mastered the emotional weaknesses that were holding me back. I'm taking a leap of faith into the unknown of individualism. You truly are a remarkable person.

What keeps me at peace now is living my true self. I trace it back to reach for my dreams. Tunnel Vision toward the future while healing from my present. I am mentally over the past, living entirely as a whole being. My present only grows stronger and in my maturity as every blink of an eye is a second closer to seeing my visions of the future. I am smiling and moving forward. Being jealous is a broken person's disease. I'm healthy and wealthy by grace. I'm turning my pain into prosperity. The body that carries me has a shell of God's armor rebuilt with Teflon metal. I'm hollow, but I'm uplifted mentally to push through any circumstance I have or will face. My courage is fear and fire purified by my commitment to the Kaan design of life. I'm living in my true present to make a change in the world, especially in my own world. We can't use all my experiences to raise awareness of living in disbelief. I am mentally and physically, and soulfully at peace. The Reapers of my life are God's doing to rebuild me. The world outside of my soul has caused me to rejoice in spiritual awareness. Are there any spirituality centers or churches to help people through the guidance of their spiritual gifts in conjunction with their faith of choice in religion? The scriptures ask this question as well,

9 For this reason, since the day we heard about you, we have not stopped praying for you. We continually ask God to fill you with the knowledge of his will through all the wisdom and understanding that the Spirit gives,

10 so that you may live a life worthy of the Lord and please him in every way: bearing fruit in every good work, growing in the knowledge of God. Colossians 1: 9-10

Do not conform to the pattern of this world but be transformed by the renewing of your mind. Then you will be able to test and approve what God's will is—his good, pleasing and perfect will. Romans 12:2

Do not bring sorrow to God's Holy Spirit by the way you live. Remember, he has identified you as his own, guaranteeing that you will be saved on the day of redemption. Ephesians 4:30

. . .

So, I say, let the Holy Spirit guide your lives. Then you won't be doing what your sinful nature craves. The sinful nature wants to do evil, which is just the opposite of what the Spirit wants. And the Spirit gives us desires that are the opposite of what sinful nature desires. These two forces are constantly fighting each other, so you are not free to carry out your good intentions. Galatians 5:16 -17

13 Which things also we speak, not in the words which man's wisdom teaches, but which the Holy Ghost teacheth; comparing spiritual things with spiritual. 1 Corinthians 2:13

Therefore, as the Holy Spirit says:
    "Today, if you will hear His voice,
    Do not harden your hearts as in the rebellion,
    On the day of trial in the wilderness,
    Where your fathers tested Me, tried Me,
    And saw My work for forty years.
    Therefore, I was angry with that generation,
    And said, 'They always go astray in their heart,
    And they have not known My ways.'
    So I swore in My wrath,
    'They shall not enter My rest.'"
Beware, brethren, lest there be in any of you an evil heart of unbelief in departing from the living God; 13 but [a]exhort one another daily, while it is called "Today," lest any of you be hardened through the deceitfulness of sin. For we have become partakers of Christ if we hold the beginning of our confidence steadfast to the end, 15 while it is said:
    "Today, if you will hear His voice,
    Do not harden your hearts as in the rebellion."

· · ·

For who, having heard, rebelled? Indeed, was it not all who came out of Egypt, led by Moses? Now with whom was He angry forty years? Was it not with those who sinned, whose corpses fell in the wilderness? 18 And to whom did He swear that they would not enter His rest, but to those who did not obey? 19 So we see that they could not enter because of unbelief. Hebrews 3: 7-19

XXV. THE ENDINGS BRING NEW BEGINNINGS

From the start, I discovered how different I am from the flock. Born with an innate curiosity for life's meaning and a desire to search for questions left unanswered, I chose to be a student of life. Life became defined by how one follows spiritual gifts. Eventually, my adventurous lifestyle revealed my true nature. I fought first in the war, which was my home life. Making it through victorious, I knew then that nothing could stop me from finding true peace in this existence.

I did not conform to anything outside of my own purpose in life. Instead, I dug deeper into how I felt and then suppressed it to overcome my battles through logic rather than emotions. Quickly, Astrology and daily awareness adapted as my key influences and the compass of my life. As I began losing everything material, I chose not to let the obstacles overtake me. Soon the absence of self-love was blocked from me mentally. I became hollow, giving in to trusting the process of Divine timing, controlled by God. I became patient, choosing to wait on God and following my knowledge of intuitive gifts. In the awakening stage of my life, I became what I lost.

This life cycle repeated until the lesson was learned. Once I decided to allow God full control over my life, He bestowed upon me the four distinctive gifts I now apply to my life daily: Clairaudience, Clairvoyance, Clairsentience, and Claircognizance. These gifts are connected to my physical, human senses, granting me the ability to hear wisdom and see visions, and receive messages from the Earth as it communicates back to me. As I continue to heal soulfully, I enhance the awareness of what I feel, adapting and appealing to those things that bring me happiness and mental health. My best gift is the cognitive growth in knowing that all things are possible and the bad can be overturned for good in my life. I chose to retrieve my passion.

So, through the journey captured in my journal, I write what is perceived as my present. I am not where I used to be. I have changed for the betterment of myself. With the ability of God's gifts, I seek to share my life as a message. I wish to teach how powerful it is to have faith. Not everyone has the same gifts, and some can never be blessed with them all at once. But I am here to assist others in becoming aware, sharing my life experiences so they can relate and press forward to the better life God has designed for them. I am a mentor for the world. This is my devotion to God's greatest blessing. So many have refused the chance to heal. That chance consists solely of learning life and what you're on this Earth to be. The design you have from God. And to realize no other human can have control over another.

I announce loudly and with pride that the best thing anyone can do with their life is to allow God to enter at any stage. Keep the faith and know that peace is coming to you. Hold yourself accountable as you allow God to drive you toward your destiny. As I have shared throughout the chapters of my memories, I desire to live a fruitful life. The Wheel of Fortune has rested on ending the pain my flesh has suffered. My soul has been saved as the faith of my seed has blossomed. I am no longer looking back on my past. Instead, I've concluded that what I endured was only to reveal how much God is needed daily. What you have learned in life can only be advice to those that need a physical example. When they see you, they will see the light of God that each and every person should carry.

We all owe Him to speak positivity through the trials that life throws at us. These are the stories where I learned how to live life through every exhale, appreciate every sunrise, and believe in every prayer. By 38, I finally reached this point. It's never too late or too soon to bring forth your study of life. The world needs healing.

I hope my memories reach each nation and are translated into every tongue. To everyone, I wish you the best that life can be.